WEAVING THE DANCE

NAVAJO YEIBICHAI TEXTILES (1910-1950)

Rebecca M. Valette

Jean-Paul Valette

Adobe Gallery
Albuquerque, New Mexico

in association with

University of Washington Press
Seattle and London

Design by Nathalie M. Valette

Photography of the weavings in the collection by Stephen Vedder,
Boston College Audiovisual Services, with the assistance of Michal Hardoof-Raz.

ISBN: 0-9633710-2-9

Library of Congress Cataloguing-in-Publication Data
Valette, Rebecca M.
Weaving the dance: Navajo Yeibichai textiles (1910-1950)/Rebecca M. Valette, Jean-Paul Valette
p. cm.
Includes bibliographical references.
ISBN 0-9633710-2-9 (pbk.)
1. Navajo textile fabrics. 2. Navajo Indians—Rites and ceremonies. I. Valette, Jean-Paul. II. Title.

E99.N3 V35 2000
746.7'2'041—dc21

00-032780

This catalog was written to accompany the exhibit:
Weaving the Dance: The Yeibichai Tradition in Navajo Rugs (1910-1950)
Museum of Our National Heritage
Lexington, Massachusetts
April 8 to September 10, 2000

Published by:
Adobe Gallery
413 Romero Street NW
Albuquerque, NM 87104
(505) 243-8485 (800) 821-5221

Distributed by:
University of Washington Press
P.O. Box 50096
Seattle, WA 98145
(206) 543-4050 (800) 441-4114

Printed by:
Puritan Press, Inc.
Hollis, NH 03049

Contents

Preface

Since its establishment in 1975, the Scottish Rite Masonic Museum of Our National Heritage in Lexington, Massachusetts, has presented temporary exhibits featuring Native American culture as an on-going component of its programs of exhibition and interpretation. These exhibits dealing with the history and art of the southwestern United States have continued to attract a wide audience. The great interest in Native American culture, both historically and today, may be in part attributed to exhibitions like "Weaving the Dance: The Yeibichai Tradition in Navajo Rugs, 1910-1950," which explores the story of a traditional sacred dance as interpreted in a twentieth century, non-traditional craft that was established for the Anglo tourist market.

"Weaving the Dance" is an exhibition of Navajo pictorial textiles, guest curated by Rebecca and Jean-Paul Valette, recognized collectors and scholars of this medium. The exhibit is drawn from their extensive collection of weavings, gathered over a 20-year period of travel and research. The more than 40 examples in this exhibit provide an inspiring look into the sacred dance traditions, oral history, and timeless weaving techniques of the Navajos. Produced by Navajo women for the local tourist market, the rugs also present a facet of the economics of many Native American groups who, confronted with the need to support themselves, made use of the popular demand for their cultural materials.

The Museum of Our National Heritage is proud to present this colorful and captivating look at the Yeibichai dance in Navajo rug weaving. We hope it will open a new window for you to one of the many twentieth century crafts of the Navajo culture that have become a meaningful part of our nation's current collecting interests.

John H. Ott
Executive Director
Museum of Our National Heritage

Foreword

Weaving the Dance is the first book to focus exclusively on the early development of a special category of twentieth-century Navajo textiles known as Yeibichai weavings. These weavings, which began to be produced around 1910, are artistic interpretations of the sacred Yeibichai dance that provides a spectacular conclusion to the nine-day Navajo ceremony called the Nightway. In spite of their theme, Yeibichai textiles were never intended for ceremonial use, but were produced exclusively for sale to an Anglo clientele willing to pay premium prices for them. Like other textiles featuring ceremonial figures, their appearance in the first decade of the twentieth century represented a major departure from Navajo traditions. Stylistically, they were quite different from the geometric, nonrepresentational type of textiles for which Navajo weavers had become famous. More significantly, the portrayal of the performers of a sacred ritual, even if done for purely secular reasons, represented a clear transgression of a widely held belief that sacred figures should not be reproduced outside of a ceremonial context. Weavers who produced them did so at the urging of traders who saw a lucrative market for this type of exotic weaving.

Because of their rarity and their intriguing theme, the first Navajo weavings to feature stylized ceremonial figures in their designs captured the imagination of wealthy collectors. William Randolph Hearst, for example, purchased two such rugs to complement his extensive collection of classic (pre-1870) Navajo blankets. By the 1930s, however, scholars were dismissing these weavings as bad examples of tourist art and writing them off as a "passing fad." Despite this dire prediction, weavings with ceremonial figures continued to be produced and now constitute a recognized and well-established category of Navajo textiles.

Today, early Yeibichai weavings are appreciated not for their ceremonial themes, but for their originality, beauty and relative scarcity. The first part of this book describes the historical and cultural background in which these weavings originated. It also traces their stylistic evolution from the highly original and complex designs created in the 1910-1935 period, to the more standardized patterns which emerged in the late 1930s and 1940s. The development of the genre is illustrated in the second part of the book by over forty examples of weavings from the 1910-1950 period.

The textiles presented here were the subject of a special exhibit held at the Museum of Our National Heritage in Lexington, Massachusetts, from April 8, 2000, to September 10, 2000. We would like to thank the museum and Executive Director John Ott for their support and encouragement. In particular, we would like to express our appreciation to Cheryl Robertson who initiated the project, Anne Starr who saw it through, Michael Rizzo who artfully created the exhibit, Maureen Harper and Tom Keaney who handled the technical details, and the members of the Burlington Quilters Guild who graciously volunteered their time to assist in the preparation of the weavings. In addition, we would like to thank Timothy Sullivan for his careful review of the manuscript, Stephen Vedder for his photography work, and most importantly Nathalie Valette who designed and produced this book.

Rebecca and Jean-Paul Valette

Part One

The Yeibichai Theme in Navajo Weavings

Brief Historical Background

The Navajos, or Diné as they call themselves, are relative newcomers to the Southwest. Of Athabascan origin, like the Apaches, they migrated in successive groups from northwest Canada during the fourteenth and fifteenth centuries and first settled along the San Juan River in northeastern New Mexico. Upon their arrival in these new lands, they came into contact with the Pueblos who were living in adobe villages in the Rio Grande valley, and from whom they learned agricultural techniques.

The first Europeans to enter the Southwest were the members of the Coronado expedition who arrived from Mexico in 1540 in a futile search for gold, plundering and destroying many Pueblo villages on their passage. About sixty years later, in 1598, another expedition, led by Juan de Oñate, brought the first Spanish settlers into the Rio Grande valley. In the ensuing years, the colonists conquered the Pueblo villages and forcibly converted their inhabitants to the Catholic faith. They failed, however, to subjugate the nomadic Navajo warriors who offered stiff resistance to Spanish incursions into their territory. In retaliatory raids against the settlers' haciendas, the Navajos acquired horses which enabled them to increase their mobility.

In 1680, the Pueblo people successfully rebelled against their Spanish conquerors, expelling them from New Mexico. Twelve years later, however, the Spaniards returned in force to repossess the Pueblo villages, with the exception of the more distant and well protected Hopi mesas. Pueblo refugees from the Rio Grande valley, fleeing the brutal Spanish repression, found shelter among the Navajos and intermarried with them. As a result of these contacts, the Navajos began to develop a new economy and way of life based on raising sheep and trading in wool and blankets.

During the eighteenth century, the Navajos gradually migrated farther westward into Arizona settling in and around Canyon de Chelly. After a period of relative peace, hostilities between the Spanish-speaking settlers and the Navajos erupted once again at the beginning of the nineteenth century. In 1805, a Spanish expedition entered the Canyon de Chelly and massacred unarmed Navajo women, children and elderly. Over the next fifty years, slave raids against the Navajos increased as the area shifted from Spanish to Mexican jurisdiction (1821) and then was annexed by the United States (1848). Increasingly concerned by the depletion of their population, the Navajos fought back against their aggressors: New Mexican ranchers to the south, and roving bands of Utes to the north.

In an effort to establish peace in the area, a number of treaties were signed between the U.S. Government and the Navajos, but these were quickly ignored or broken by both parties. In 1851, the U.S. Army built Fort Defiance deep in Navajo territory in an attempt to "pacify" the population. In 1860, a band of one thousand Navajo warriors launched an unsuccessful attack on the fort in response to the soldiers' encroachment on their grazing lands.

As the Civil War spread to the New Mexico Territory, General James H. Carleton, commander of the Union forces, decided to solve the "Navajo problem" once and for all by launching a massive military campaign against the native population. In the summer of 1863, Army troops, under the command of Colonel Kit Carson, invaded the Canyon de Chelly and the surrounding lands, systematically destroying the homes, fields, orchards, food caches and sheep herds of the fleeing Navajos. After a few months of such scorched earth tactics, the Navajos, driven by starvation and the bitter cold of winter, began surrendering in small groups. More than 9,000 captive men, women and children were forced

Figure 1. *Navajo weaver. Photograph by Ben Wittick, ca. 1890.*

to march 300 miles eastward to Fort Sumner, New Mexico, to a camp known as Bosque Redondo. Many died on that Long Walk, and many more perished over the next four years as a result of the miserable conditions at the internment camp. Finally, in 1868, a peace treaty was negotiated and the Navajos were allowed to return to their native lands where they were granted a Reservation of their own. Slowly the native sheep herds were reconstituted, and the population once more began to expand. By 1900, the Navajos numbered over 15,000 and their Reservation lands had been doubled in size.

The Tradition of Navajo Weaving

Weaving is an essential part of Navajo culture and its only traditional art form. According to an ancestral legend, the Navajos were taught the art of weaving by Spider Woman, a supernatural being who showed them how to set up and string their looms. The Navajos did know how to weave baskets prior to their migration to the Southwest and perhaps had a rudimentary knowledge of weaving textiles. They learned more sophisticated weaving techniques from the Pueblos, to whom they gave shelter after the brutal Spanish reconquest at the end of the seventeenth century. Navajo women quickly became recognized as experts in the craft, surpassing their Pueblo mentors in the technical and artistic quality of their weaving. They made beautifully designed blankets for their own use and also for trade with other tribes.

Weaving substantially declined between 1864 and 1868, when the Navajos were forcibly relocated to the Bosque Redondo internment camp. Because they had lost most of their sheep herds and all means of subsistence, they were issued Western clothing and coarse Rio Grande blankets. Weaving for personal use almost disappeared in the years following the Navajos' return to their newly-created Reservation, since they could purchase comfortable and inexpensive machine-made "Pendleton" trade blankets.

The weaving craft was revived in the last quarter of the nineteenth century when traders who had established posts on or near the Reservation encouraged Navajo women to create weavings for sale to the Anglo market: warm blankets in handspun yarns reviving traditional geometric designs; light and very colorful blankets woven in commercial "Germantown" yarns ; and later, durable rugs with full borders and fanciful center fields with designs reminiscent of Oriental and Caucasian carpets. The early years of the twentieth century witnessed the blossoming of a wide variety of styles of Navajo weaving, and the birth of the Yeibichai weavings.

The Navajo Spiritual Universe and Ceremonial System

Figure 2. *Yeibichai dancers in a brush enclosure. Photograph by P. Clinton Bortell, ca. 1919.*

Traditional Navajos are a deeply spiritual people. Many acts of their daily life contain a sacred dimension and must be performed in a specific way to maintain balance and harmony between the self and the other elements of a complex universe. This universe includes all the multiple aspects of the visible world: its people, animals, plants, natural formations, weather phenomena and celestial objects. It also includes an almost infinite number of powerful supernatural beings and divinities generally known as Holy People who, according to the Navajo Creation Story, emerged onto the surface of the Earth from different levels of a subterranean world. The Holy People then reshaped the Earth and made it fit for living. They also created the Navajos in their own image, taught them basic survival skills and gave them a code of behavior so that they could live in harmony with the universe.

While harmony brings with it beauty, blessedness and a general sense of well-being, its disruption, brought about by improper behavior, causes illness with a broad range of physical, mental and emotional symptoms. To reestablish harmony and its beneficial effects or, conversely, to cure the ill effects resulting from disrupted harmony, the Navajos depend on an elaborate system of ceremonies conducted under the close supervision of highly trained medicine men or Singers. The aim of a Navajo curative ritual is to attract the Holy People to the scene of the ceremony so that they might bestow their benevolent powers on a patient whose harmony has been willfully or accidentally disrupted. The most powerful rite in the ceremony is the sandpainting, which is created by drawing the images of these Holy People on a flat sand surface using various mineral pigments. When the patient sits on the completed sandpainting, he or she becomes identified with these divinities and is filled by their goodness; at the same time, evil is chased out and harmony is restored. At the end of the rite, the sandpainting is ritually destroyed and the sand ceremonially disposed of.

The Nightway and the Yeibichai Dance

One of the major Navajo curative ceremonies, the Nightway, invokes the Yeis, a special category of Holy People who are generally well disposed toward the Navajos, and their leader, who is called Yeibichai or Talking God. A Nightway ceremony lasts nine days and can be performed only during the frosty months of the year when the snakes are hibernating and the danger of lightning has disappeared.

The Nightway is unique in that the Yeis appear during the actual ceremony, impersonated by masked and ceremonially attired Navajos. On the ninth and final night of the ceremony, these god-impersonators appear in a public performance, commonly referred to as the Yeibichai Dance. A Yeibichai dance team consists of fourteen god-impersonators: six Male and six Female Yeis; their leader Yeibichai, or Talking God; and Water Sprinkler, the God of Precipitated Waters, who does not actually perform the dance steps but provides comic relief during the performance.

The Yeibichai Dance attracts hundreds, and occasionally thousands, of Navajos who travel long distances to benefit from the presence of the divinities. Throughout the night, teams of masked god-impersonators from various parts of the Reservation relay each other, performing dance steps according to a prescribed ritual. The dancing continues until just before dawn, when the Nightway ceremony concludes with the chanting of the "Bluebird Song" in celebration of the peace and happiness that this bird symbolizes.

Early Iconography of the Yeibichai Dance

In the early 1880s, American ethnologists began studying Navajo ceremonies, a field of research that had not yet attracted the attention of scholars. Washington Matthews, a military surgeon posted at Fort Wingate, Arizona, who acted as a unpaid correspondent for the recently established American Bureau of Ethnology, witnessed his first Yeibichai dance in December 1880. In the ensuing years, he conducted extensive field research on the Nightway ceremony and, in 1902, published a composite account of the ceremony which to this date remains the basic reference text on the subject. In 1885, James Stevenson, a field worker for the Bureau of Ethnology, attended a nine-day Nightway ceremony and recorded his observations in a lengthy article which became the first published account of the ceremony. In their reports on the Nightway, Matthews and Stevenson gave detailed descriptions of the Yeibichai dance, the ritual attire of the dancers and sequence of the dance movements, but did not provide illustrations of the dancers or their performances.

Possibly the first sketch of a Yeibichai dance was done in 1902 by Apie Begay, a Navajo from Chaco Canyon who regularly assisted medicine men during Nightway ceremonies. At the invitation of Kenneth Chapman, an ethnologist working in the area who provided him with paper and crayons, Apie Begay drew a picture of Talking God and two Male Yeis (Fig. 3).

Figure 3. *Talking God and two Male Yei dancers. Drawing by Apie Begay, 1902. School of American Research, Santa Fe, NM.*

Figure 4. *Navajo men posing as Yeibichai dancers. Photograph by Edward S. Curtis, 1904.*

In the spring of 1904, Edward Sheriff Curtis, the well-known portrait photographer from Seattle who had set for himself the mission of publishing a visual record of all the Native tribes west of the Mississippi, went to the Navajo Reservation for the explicit purpose of photographing different aspects of a Nightway ceremony. Shortly after his arrival in Canyon de Chelly, Curtis realized not only that the winter ceremonial season had passed, but also that the Navajos of the area were so strongly opposed to having their ceremonies recorded that his project would be impossible to realize under any circumstances. Undaunted by these seemingly insurmountable difficulties, Curtis asked the local trader to recruit Navajos willing to dress as Nightway participants and reenact a few steps of the Yeibichai dance. Although the photographs are staged and, therefore, do not provide a record of an actual ceremony, they do show the postures and accouterments of the dancers with a substantial degree of realism (Fig. 4).

The following year another photographer, Simeon Schwemberger, took pictures of parts of a Nightway ceremony near St. Michaels, Arizona, with the consent of the officiating medicine man. Although Schwemberger did not photograph the Yeibichai dance itself, most probably because of the technical difficulties of photographing at night, his pictures do show the ritual accouterments of Talking God and other god impersonators in their various roles during the Nightway ceremony (cf. Long 1992:39-75).

In 1908, Stewart Culin, the curator of the Brooklyn Museum, visited the Southwest and collected a colored drawing of Yeibichai dancers drawn by a Navajo student at Mother Catherine's School at St. Michaels, Arizona (Fig. 5; cf. Fane et al 1991:54, 58). Around the same time, Klah-so (Big Lefthanded), a Navajo from Tuba City, painted a Yeibichai scene on a piece of brown cloth (Parezo 1983:55). The photographs of Curtis and Schwemberger, and the drawings of Apie Begay, Klah-so and the St. Michaels' school boy probably constitute the earliest pictorial documents of the Yeibichai dance.[1]

Figure 5. *Talking God and four Male Yei dancers. Drawing by a Navajo student at St. Michaels, AZ, 1908. Brooklyn Museum.*

Figure 6. *Sixteen-figure scene of a Yeibichai dance. Carvings by Clitso Dedman, ca. 1945. California Academy of Sciences, San Francisco.*

Perhaps the most evocative rendition of a Yeibichai dance as it was performed at the turn of the twentieth century is provided by the carvings of Clitso Dedman, generally considered to be the first Navajo carver to have reached commercial status (Valette and Valette, 2000). An extraordinarily gifted and unconventional man, Clitso Dedman began carving in the early 1940s when he was in his sixties, in spite of a well-established Navajo tradition that frowned upon the carved reproduction of human, and even more importantly sacred, figures. Over a thirteen-year period, Clitso produced about thirty large 16-piece sets of Yeibichai dancers which were marketed to Anglo collectors by his friend and mentor Cozy McSparron, the innovative trader at Chinle. Because of Clitso Dedman's insistence on accuracy, his carvings provide a generally realistic portrayal of the ritual attire worn by Yeibichai dancers in ceremonies that he would have witnessed in his youth, as well as a three-dimensional representation of their stances. The scene in Figure 6 captures the moment of the Nightway ceremony when a team of Yeibichai dancers appears on the dance ground to be greeted by the Medicine Man, to the left of the group, and the Patient, standing next to him. Led by Talking God, the dancers appear in single file with alternating Male and Female Yeis. Bringing up the rear of the dance line is Water Sprinkler. In Clitso Dedman's carvings, the female divinities are impersonated not by women but by men, as was generally the ceremonial custom in Yeibichai dances around 1900. Except for some details that have been omitted in the ritual decoration of the masks, the figures of the god-impersonators are accurately represented.

Talking God

Talking God is the leader of the Yeis. His impersonator wears a white headmask topped with a fantail of twelve eagle feathers. Around his neck, he wears a green ruff of spruce twigs. Other ceremonial items include a broad white deerskin sash draped across his torso and knotted over his left shoulder and an Abert squirrel pelt which he holds in the right hand. He is otherwise wearing the everyday attire of a traditional Navajo man, consisting of a long-sleeved shirt and calico pants.

Figure 7. *Water Sprinkler, Male Yei, Female Yei, and Talking God. Carvings by Clitso Dedman, ca. 1945.*

Male Yeis

Male Yei impersonators wear full headmasks, blue in front and white in back, and topped with two eagle feathers. The mouth of each mask is fitted with the neck of a gourd that serves as a breathing pipe. The dancers wear short colorful kilts, heavy concha belts with kit-fox pelts dangling down the back, blue leggings held up below the knee by red woolen garters, and moccasins decorated with large silver buttons. Their torsos, arms and thighs are smeared with white clay. Other ceremonial items include spruce ruffs around their necks, gourd rattles held in their right hands, and bunches of spruce twigs or feathers held in their left hands.

Female Yeis

The Female Yeis wear blue square masks that cover only their faces, allowing their long black hair to flow freely over their shoulders and down their backs. There are no spruce ruffs around their necks. In their hands, they carry bunches of spruce twigs or feathers, but no gourd rattles. When the Female Yeis are impersonated by men, as in this set of carvings, their attire is otherwise identical to that of the Male Yeis. When they are impersonated by women, however, Female Yeis wear traditional dresses with red sashes and white deerskin leggings.

Water Sprinkler

Water Sprinkler is the Navajo "God of Precipitated Waters." In the Yeibichai dance, his impersonator provides comic relief as the clown, clumsily imitating the movements of the performers. Dressed like a Male Yei, he also wears juniper bracelets on his arms and wrists, and longer juniper garlands across his torso. In his right hand he carries a kit-fox pelt which he twirls around in mimicry of Talking God. In some Nightway performances, Water Sprinkler wears a long-sleeved shirt and long pants rather than a kilt and body paint.

Weavings with Ceremonial Themes: Yei, Yeibichai and Sandpainting Textiles

Sometime in the 1860s, a Navajo woman wove a highly decorative blanket in the design of which she inserted a small figure representing a Holy Person or Yei, possibly from the Windway ceremony (Blomberg 1990). This blanket, formerly in the William Randolph Hearst collection and now in the Southwest Museum in Los Angeles, is the earliest known Navajo textile to feature a ceremonial figure. Other examples dating back to the 1890s are extremely rare and poorly documented. Their origins, the identities of their weavers, and the reasons why they were woven remain mysteries.

The commercial development of weavings with ceremonial figures did not begin until the early years of the twentieth century when traders encouraged weavers to make this novel and exotic type of Navajo textile as they saw a lucrative market for them. Dick Simpson, an English immigrant who had established a trading post along the Gallegos Wash some ten miles southeast of Farmington, New Mexico, is generally credited with having initiated the process around 1905. One of his best weavers was his young Navajo wife, Yah-nah-pah who wove four blankets featuring large ceremonial figures before she died in 1913 at the age of twenty-four (Valette and Valette, 1997).

In spite of their religious themes, Navajo textiles with ceremonial figures were never intended for ceremonial use. They were secular objects, produced exclusively for sale to a clientele of Anglo tourists willing to pay premium prices for them. Nevertheless, their initial appearance provoked a strong negative reaction in the Navajo community. The reason was that the weaving of such textiles constituted a direct transgression of a widely held traditional belief that prohibited the reproduction of sacred figures in a permanent form and outside of a ceremonial context. Not surprisingly, relatively few weavers engaged in their production which probably amounted to no more than one per cent of the total output of Navajo textiles during the 1900-1950 period.

As time passed, the Navajo culture evolved, especially as a result of World War II when many young Navajo men and women temporarily left the Reservation to join the armed forces or work in the armament industry. As Navajo traditional beliefs and restrictions progressively lost their power, the production of textiles with ceremonial figures became judged with less severity. By the 1960s such textiles had become an integral part of the vast catalogue of different styles of Navajo weavings. They continue to be produced today, although many traditional weavers still show reluctance to make them.

The terminology by which the various types of weavings ceremonial figures are designated, has been fluid for many decades. Early traders tended to refer to any weaving with ceremonial figures as a "Yei" rug, whether it depicted the Holy People or their human impersonators. The term "Yeibichai" rug was also used to describe to both styles, as well as to reproductions of sandpaintings from the Nightway since the Navajos commonly refer to that ceremony as a "Yeibichai." Today most scholars, collectors and dealers have adopted the following classification of weavings with ceremonial figures.

- **Yei weavings** represent the Yei divinities and other Holy People, usually depicted as a row of identical figures.
- **Yeibichai weavings** represent the human beings who impersonate the Yeis as they perform the Yeibichai dance.
- **Sandpainting weavings** represent the Holy People in complex configurations inspired by the actual sandpaintings created during Navajo ceremonies.

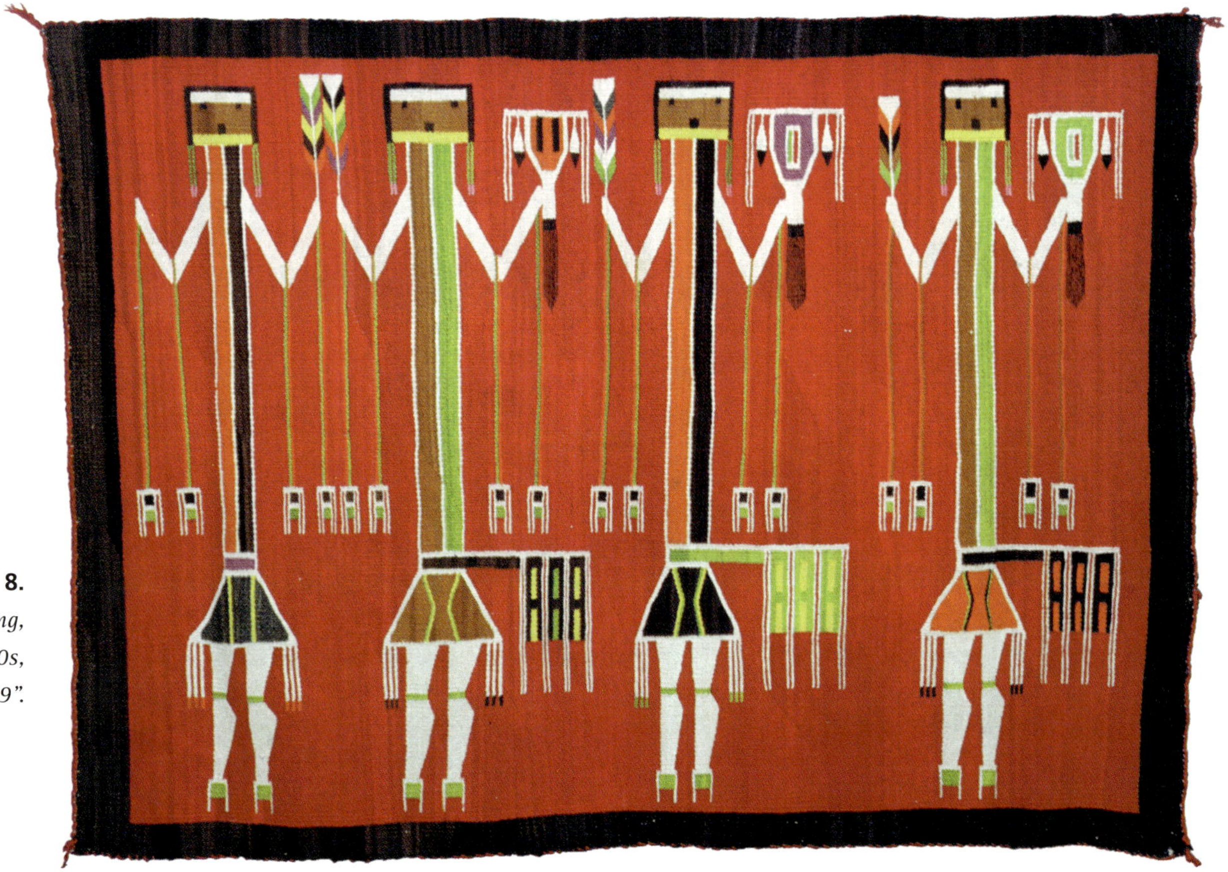

Figure 8.
Yei weaving, 1930s, 43" x 59".

Exact statistics on the relative production of each category do not exist. Yei weavings are by far the largest category of Navajo textiles with ceremonial figures and may account for 85% of the total output, with Yeibichai and Sandpainting weavings representing 15% and 5%, respectively.

In spite of some similarities, Yei and Yeibichai weavings are stylistically quite different. In Yei weavings, the divinities are pictured as highly stylized figures with slim elongated bodies in an erect, frozen posture (Fig. 8). In the Yeibichai weavings, on the other hand, the dancers exhibit the features of actual human beings and are represented in motion (Fig. 9). The Male Yeis are usually shown wearing blue leggings and red moccasins. Because the weaver must reproduce the shape and contours of the human body using the interplay of horizontal, vertical and diagonal lines, and also convey the movement of the dance on a two-dimensional medium, Yeibichai weavings are technically much more challenging to produce than their Yei counterparts. At the same time, they lend themselves to a much greater variety of designs. Because of their originality, beauty and relative rarity, the early examples are sought after by collectors.

Figure 9. *Yeibichai weaving, 1920s, 35" x 75".*

Well aware of the traditional prohibition against the reproduction of sacred figures and fearing the possible divine retribution that its transgression could bring on themselves and their families, the early Navajo weavers were very careful not to produce exact representations of the Holy People. Instead they created highly imaginative renditions of the divinities by omitting essential details or by adding fictitious elements. Similarly, when portraying the human beings who impersonate the Yei divinities in the Yeibichai dance, Navajo weavers were equally careful not to represent too accurately certain aspects of their ceremonial attire, notably the sacred masks that make them divine. Some weavers, however, often working under the direction of Medicine Men, produced very accurate representations of actual sandpaintings, so as to preserve these designs for future generations. In the 1920s and 1930s Hosteen Klah, himself a famous Medicine Man, wove careful copies of the sandpaintings of the Nightway and other ceremonies in which he was specialized, either alone or in cooperation with his two nieces (Newcomb 1964). Atlnaba, the daughter of Manuelito, a Shootingway singer, wove reproductions of the sandpaintings of that ceremony (Reichard 1934). Aside from these rare exceptions, weavings with ceremonial designs should be considered only as artistic and fanciful interpretations of sacred images made for profit by craftswomen very well aware of the distinction between the secular and the sacred.

Historical and Stylistic Development of Yeibichai Weaving (1900-1950)

Given the lack of appropriate documentation, the precise origins of Yeibichai weavings cannot be determined. There is, however, enough indirect evidence, such as photographs, museum accession records, and miscellaneous correspondence, to formulate a general picture of the evolution of the genre from its emergence at the beginning of the twentieth century until it became firmly established as a distinctive category of Navajo weaving in the late 1940s.

Origin and Early Development (1900-1915)

Whereas Navajo textiles including stylized representations of Holy People can be traced as far back as the 1860s, there is no documented evidence of any Yeibichai weavings prior to 1900. The earliest known blankets to incorporate Yeibichai dancers in their design exhibit the style and technical characteristics of Navajo textiles woven at the turn of the twentieth century. An outstanding example of this type is a four-ply Germantown blanket in the Elkus Collection at the California Academy of Sciences in San Francisco (Fig. 10). Woven in a "Moki revival" pattern, this textile features two pairs of small but well-delineated male and female dancers against a background of alternating black and purple stripes. The Moki revival pattern was originated in the 1890s by John Lorenzo Hubbell, the Ganado trader, and weavings in this style continued to be produced until 1910 and possibly beyond; therefore, without accurate records of provenance, precise dating of the Elkus blanket remains problematic.

In the blanket on the right, and other related examples, figures of Yeibichai dancers are used as secondary decorative elements. Weavings featuring Yeibichai figures as their primary

Figure 10. *Partial view of a Moki revival Germantown blanket with two pairs of Yeibichai dancers, 1890-1910, 55" x 99". California Academy of Sciences, San Francisco.*

Figure 11. *Weaving with a single Yeibichai dancer, by Yah-nah-pah, ca. 1910, 51" x 77". Notah Dineh, Cortez, CO.*

Figure 12. *Weaving with two Yeibichai dancers shown in profile, ca. 1910, 46" x 61". Stark Museum of Art, Orange, TX.*

motif probably appeared shortly before 1910. A blanket depicting a large and fancifully attired dancer, facing forward, was woven around that time by Yah-nah-pah, the talented Navajo wife of Dick Simpson, the Gallegos Canyon trader credited by most scholars as having initiated the commercial development of weavings with ceremonial figures (Fig. 11). Another early blanket, now at the Stark Museum in Orange, Texas, features two realistically portrayed dancers shown in profile (Fig. 12). Because of strong technical resemblance with the preceding blanket, and a similar stepped sawtooth border, this textile could possibly have also been woven by Yah-nah-pah, or another early Gallegos Canyon weaver, and therefore would also bear a circa-1910 date.

In the absence of contrary information, it may be assumed that the more complex Yeibichai textiles featuring single rows of several dancers did not begin to be woven until the early 1910s.[2] However, over the course of the decade there must have been a number of weavers producing rugs of this type since by 1920, the Yeibichai style was firmly established.

Creative Phase (1915-1935)

Historical photographs indicate that the Yei, Yeibichai, and Sandpainting styles of weaving were regularly produced by the early 1920s. Pictures taken at the first Santa Fe Indian Fair in 1922 show the three categories of weavings with ceremonial figures prominently displayed among more conventional Navajo textiles of the period. The two Yeibichai rugs in Figure 13 (top right and center right) exhibit a fully mature design. Both rugs feature teams of dancers, led by Talking God and consisting of unevenly alternating male and female Yei-impersonators. Water Sprinkler, rarely represented in Yeibichai weavings, is pictured in the center rug. In both weavings, the dance scenes are framed by intricate geometric borders in a style typical of the period.

While the various categories of Navajo weaving with ceremonial figures developed together, their individual stylistic evolution took different paths. The Yei blanket was popularized and heavily marketed after World War I by Will Evans, trader at Shiprock, who decorated the exterior walls of his trading post and a nearby lodge with rows of Yei figures, thus giving the weavers of his area a basic model to reproduce. As a result, Yei textiles were woven according to a fairly standard pattern which many considered monotonously repetitive.

The weavers of Yeibichai rugs, on the other hand, did not have any pre-set models to follow. Consequently they relied primarily on their personal observations of the Yeibichai dance and their own sense of creativity. Not surprisingly, the period of Yeibichai weaving is characterized by an explosion of individual designs ranging from the simple and realistic to the most complex and highly imaginative. Stylistic differences involve the identity, number and size of the figures represented and the details in their ceremonial attire. Generally the weavers included Talking God as the lead figure, followed by a row of at least six dancers, consisting of men and women dancers alternating in an even or uneven sequence, in contrast with weavings of the following period where only Male Yeis are represented. The accouterments of each dancer, notably the kilts of the Male Yeis and the dresses of the women, were generally individualized in their design and color. Decorative elements such as bows, arrows, birds, rainbow bars and intertwined geometric shapes are found in the field of the rugs. Other differentiating elements include the color scheme, the design of the border and the size of the weaving. In some simple rugs, the palette is limited to the shades of natural wool, but in most instances it is enhanced by the use of brilliant colors, such as red,

Figure 13. *Partial view of the exhibit hall at the First Indian Fair in Santa Fe, New Mexico, 1922.*

orange, purple, green, and sometimes blue and yellow. The borders, which occasionally consist of a single black band, are more often formed by intricate geometric designs of intertwining lines. In size, the Yeibichai weavings range from small saddle blankets to very large pieces of over 5' x 7', often woven on commission. Technically the early Yeibichai weavings range from the coarse, especially at the beginning of the period, to the very fine. The primary material is homespun wool, sometimes supplemented by commercial Germantown yarn.

Many Yeibichai weavings of exceptional originality and technical quality were produced during the period. The best examples were marketed by the Fred Harvey Company through its outlets along the Santa Fe Railway, notably the Indian Room in Albuquerque and the Hopi House at the Grand Canyon, as well as by other stores catering to a well-heeled clientele, such as the Verkamp Curio store, also in the Grand Canyon. Not surprisingly, the originality and quality of these weavings attracted the attention of noted collectors, such as William Randolph Hearst, the newspaper magnate, Marjorie Merriwether Post, the heiress of the cereal fortune, and Thea Heye, wife of the founder of the Museum of the American Indian in New York. Yeibichai weavings were also collected during the period by a few Navajos, notably by Chee Dodge, their wealthy leader who became the first Chairman of the Navajo Tribal Council in 1923.[3]

Standardization Phase (1935-1950)

The onset of the Great Depression in the early 1930s resulted in a general reduction of tourism and a substantially lower demand for high quality, high priced native-made artifacts. By that time, the Yeibichai genre was firmly established (Reichard 1936:154) and weavers were generally aware of other styles produced in their area. As demand for cheaper and, therefore, more marketable textiles increased, simple and easy-to-reproduce patterns of Yeibichai textiles began to emerge. The standard pattern which eventually prevailed consisted of a row of six male dancers with or without Talking God represented as their leader. Female dancers, with their flared and intricately designed dresses, generally disappeared in the weavings made after 1935. In the standard pattern, the stylized male dancers, identical in every way except for minor variations in the decoration of their kilts, stand facing forward in a rigid stance. The field of the rugs is plain, without additional decorative elements such as feathers and other ornaments found in the textiles of the prior period. The simplified borders consist of a plain single or double band of color. In spite of a general decline in creativity, some Yeibichai weavings of outstanding design and craftsmanship continued to be produced. The basic pattern, however, was not substantially modified until the late 1960s and early 1970s when several talented weavers began to create new artistic interpretations of the Yeibichai dance (cf. Hedlund 1997:36-38; Rodee 1987:146-47).

---

[1] There are also several Navajo petroglyphs of Yeibichai dancers, but their dating is uncertain (cf. Shaafsma 1992:38-40).

[2] In her biography of Hosteen Klah, Franc Newcomb, an early expert on Navajo ceremonial designs, relates how the famous medicine man, best known for his weaving of accurate sandpainting rugs, made a blanket in 1911 depicting a "set of Yeibichai dancers" (Newcomb 1964:115). Given the terminology used at that time, it would appear that this early rug, whose whereabouts are today unknown, was not a Yeibichai weaving, but rather Klah's first weaving of a Whirling Logs sandpainting (cf. Coolidge and Coolidge 1932:106).

[3] In 1923, Chee Dodge presented one of his Yeibichai rugs to the Smithsonian Institute (Ortiz 1983:597).

Part Two

Yeibichai Weavings (1910-1950)

Basic Designs

While Yei rugs were usually woven around Shiprock, Yeibichai weavings were produced across the broader Four Corners area, extending from Lukachukai and Upper Greasewood in the west to the Gallegos Canyon of the "Checkerboard" Reservation in the east. According to the orientation of their figures, these early Yeibichai weavings can be classified into two groups, named after the localities which specialized in their designs. It must be remembered, however, that both styles of weavings were produced in a much wider area than their names would indicate.

- **The Lukachukai style** was the prevalent style of Yeibichai weaving in the 1910-1950 period. Lukachukai rugs are rectangular and have a horizontal orientation. They usually feature a long row of dancers, all facing forward.
- **The Gallegos style** probably originated around 1910, and remained limited to the area south of Farmington. In this style, the dancers are characteristically represented in three-quarter profile, rather than facing forward. The rugs are oriented vertically and usually have a square format featuring only two to four dancers.

By the 1940s, the Gallegos style began to increase somewhat in popularity. Certain weavers began to incorporate the profile depiction of the dancers (Gallegos style) into a horizontal orientation (Lukachukai style), laying the basis for the development of Yeibichai weavings of the 1960s and 1970s.

With the exception of the early single figure blanket-size textiles and the much more common small "Gallup throws" featuring one or two Yeibichai dancers, most Yeibichai weavings portray several dancers, usually in a single horizontal line. Due to space constraints, the weavers rarely represent all fourteen members of a Yeibichai dance team (Talking God, six Male Yeis, six Female Yeis, and Water Sprinkler), but instead include only four to ten figures. A few large weavings exhibit two teams of dancers, one above the other.

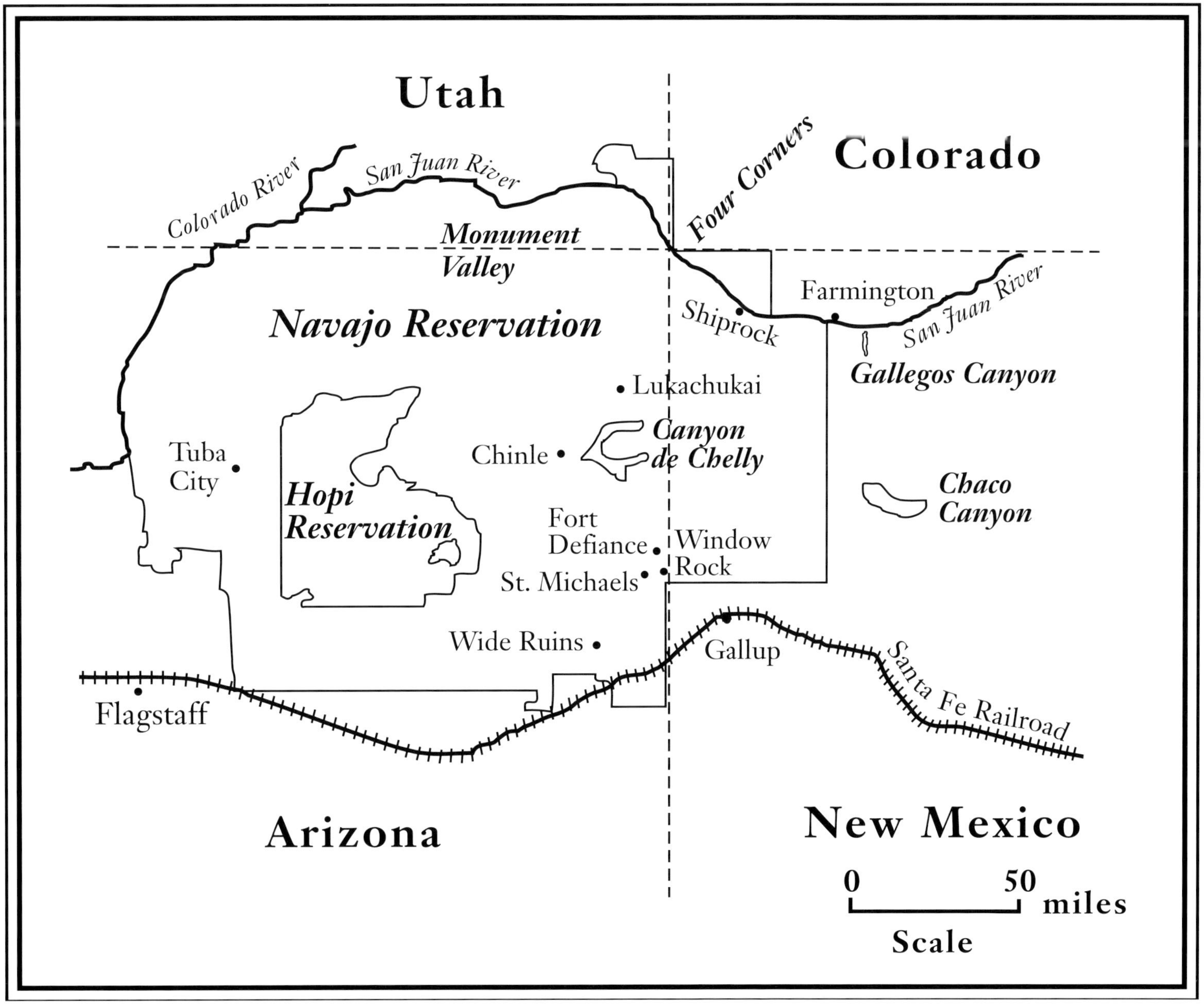

Figure 14. Map of the Navajo Reservation.

Single Yeibichai Dancers

Blanket-size weavings featuring large, single Yei-like figures as their central motif began to appear around 1905. They were created by Navajo weavers living near the Simpson Trading Post in the Gallegos Canyon, south of Farmington, New Mexico. This style received almost immediate attention from collectors as a result of the publication in 1914 of George Wharton James' book *Indian Blankets and their Makers* which contained plates featuring such weavings both in color and black-and-white (James 1914:139-142; figs. 200, 201). Because of this publicity, traders encouraged other Navajo weavers to produce adaptations, and sometimes very close imitations, of the single Yei design.

Textiles with single Yeibichai dancers also began to be woven in the same Gallegos area at about the same time. The early weavers included Dick Simpson's Navajo wife Yah-nah-pah who wove a fairly realistic representation of a dancer (see Figure 11) and her older sister Gle-nup-pah, whose renditions of the Male Yeis are much more stylized (Valette and Valette 1997). Because the single dancer style was not publicized until much later (Amsden 1934:196, plate 53) and, therefore, less prone to imitation, only few weavers produced this pattern. As a result, pre-1930 blanket-size weavings (ranging in size from 40 to 50 inches in width and 60 to 75 inches in length) that feature clearly identifiable single Yeibichai dancers are relatively rare. On the other hand, small Gallup "throws" (about 15 inches by 25 inches) decorated with male or female Yeibichai dancers are fairly common and continued to be woven much later.

1. Male Yeibichai Dancer

The weaver of this textile has created a composite picture of a Yeibichai dancer. The central figure is a Male Yei-impersonator, but he is wearing the white mask and multi-feathered headdress of Talking God. The other elements of his attire—the colorful kilt with tassel fringe, the purple woolen leggings held up by red woven garters, and the deerskin moccasins decorated with silver buttons—are typical of the dress of male dancers. The stylized creeping plant that frames the scene may be a squash vine, one of the four plants considered sacred by the Navajos.

circa 1920
61″ x 32″
warps 9
wefts 32
handspun wool

2. Single Yeibichai-style Figure

This blanket is a testimony to the artistry and creativity shown by the early Gallegos weavers who created the "Yei/Yeibichai" genre in the early 1900s. Although not in ceremonial attire, the central figure with his feathered mask is evocative of a participant in the Yeibichai dance. The objects that he holds in his hands appear to be stylized representations of the ritual gourd rattle and the bunch of juniper sprigs normally carried by the male dancers during the ceremony. The cross on his necklace, however, is a fanciful addition, possibly included by the weaver to make him look less like an actual Yei-impersonator.

circa 1910
77" x 46"
warps 9
wefts 32
handspun wool
attributed to Gle-nup-pah (1878-1925)

3. Male Yeibichai Dancer

Except for the mask, which the weaver has purposely represented in white rather than blue, this weaving provides a stylized but fairly accurate representation of a male Yeibichai dancer as he might have appeared in a Nightway ceremony at the beginning of the twentieth century. The various elements of his ceremonial attire have been rendered in great detail: the spruce ruff around his neck, his large silver concha belt, his colorful kilt adorned with dangling fringes and tassels, and the prominently displayed fox pelt hanging from the back of the belt. His torso, arms and thighs are covered with ritual white clay body paint. The dancer's feet are pointing forward, giving a realistic touch to this portrayal.

1915-1925
57″ x 38″
warps 10
wefts 26
handspun wool

4. Male Yeibichai Dancer

This stylized portrayal of a Yeibichai dancer, with its heavy use of horizontal, vertical, and diagonal lines, appears to be the work of a weaver more at ease with geometric designs than with the realistic portrayal of the human body. A thin rectangle is used to represent the spruce ruff around the dancer's neck, and zigzag lines represent his necklace. The silver-studded leather strap of his bandoleer pouch is suggested by a diagonal line of white squares. The stacks of triangles that appear as decorative elements are traditional Navajo cloud symbols. The muted palette, consisting of the natural colors of the wool and a limited use of aniline red, is typical of Navajo rugs woven in the first quarter of the twentieth century.

circa 1915
54" x 35"
warps 8
wefts 28
handspun wool

5. Saddle Blanket with Female Yeibichai dancer

With spruce twigs in her hands and her arms raised in a V, this simplified figure evokes a female Yeibichai dancer in traditional attire. She is wearing white leather leggings and a concha belt fastened over a red woven sash with green highlights. The border design of this weaving is typical of the saddle blankets woven between 1910 and 1930.

1910-1930
28″ x 30″
warps 6
wefts 24
handspun wool,
commercial yarn

Women Dancers in Yeibichai Rugs

Both Male and Female Yeis usually appear in the Yeibichai dance as they represent opposite yet complementary elements of the universe. The ethnologists who observed the ritual between 1880 and 1920 noted that the Female Yeis were generally impersonated not by women, but rather by teenage boys and men of small stature, although a woman would occasionally insert herself in the line of male dancers. The absence of women in Yeibichai dance teams was not attributed to any sexual ceremonial disqualification but to their lack of appropriate training and, more importantly, to the fear that the presence of menstruating women could bring evil rather than goodness on those in attendance. Another reason was that women and their future progeny should be protected against the potential ill effects of a ceremony not properly conducted.

In contrast to these early observations of the Nightway, a large proportion of Yeibichai weavings produced in the 1920-1935 period feature women rather than men as Female Yei impersonators. In this role, they wear the characteristic square face masks of the divinities, and hold bunches of spruce in their half-raised hands. Unlike their male counterparts, they do not wear spruce ruffs around their necks and their long hair flows freely over their shoulders. Their dress is typical of the formal attire worn by Navajo women at that time: colorful velveteen blouses and long gathered skirts, leggings made of bands of white deerskin, brown moccasins and abundant jewelry.

As is characteristic of the Yeibichai weavings of the period, the examples included in this section exhibit stylistic originality and diversity in designs with abundant variations in the number and size of the figures, the male-female alternation and the details of the ceremonial attire.

6. Yeibichai Design

The line of masked dancers featured in this weaving includes the four different Navajo divinities who are impersonated in the Yeibichai dance: Talking God in the lead, alternating Male and Female Yeis, and Water Sprinkler at the end of the dance line.

The colorful central scene is enhanced by the strong black background. The upper and lower bands are decorated with rows of Maltese crosses, a design element introduced into Navajo rugs in the 1890s.

circa 1925
67″ x 41″
warps 8
wefts 28-34
handspun wool

7. Yeibichai Dancers

1920s
84″ x 46″
warps 8
wefts 28
handspun wool

Like many early Yeibichai weavings, this rather coarsely woven rug features an uneven number of dancers and an irregular alternation of men and women. The shape of the masks, rectangular for the Female Yeis and rounded for the Male Yeis, is represented correctly, but their coloring, which should be blue, is inaccurate. The exaggerated height of some of the dancers gives this piece a fresh, naive feeling. The weaver has filled in the background with an array of sacred eagle feathers.

8. Yeibichai Dancers

The weaver of this piece has individualized each dancer by creating different designs for the dresses of the Female Yeis and the kilts of the Male Yeis. Across his chest, Talking God wears a leather bandoleer strap to which is attached a medicine pouch. His pants are woven in an unusual striped design. The feathers floating above the heads of the women dancers are fanciful decorative elements. The powerful black background evokes the night atmosphere in which the Yeibichai dance is performed.

1920s
85″ x 38″
warps 10
wefts 30
handspun wool
commercial yarn

9. Yeibichai Dancers

circa 1930
78″ x 38″
warps 8
wefts 32
handspun wool

Through her careful control of space, the weaver of this brightly colored piece was able to fit twelve dancers into her composition. These dancers are shown in their traditional stance, with the women's arms up in a V position and the men's close to the waist. The colorful attire of the dancers is enhanced by the red border of interlocking T shapes which is typical of the period.

10. Yeibichai Dancers

In this piece, the weaver has paid much more attention to composition and color than to accuracy in representing the attire of the dancers. To show the heads of the dancers on the same plane, she has raised the feet of the two shorter Female Yeis so that they seem to be stand in back of the male divinities. The stylized square faces at each end of the weaving may represent Holy People watching the dance.

circa 1925
88″ x 39″
wefts 8
warps 28
handspun wool,
commercial yarn

11. Yeibichai Dancers

circa 1925
86″ x 50″
warps 9
wefts 32
handspun wool

Except for the unusual black coloring of the masks, the weaver has represented the ceremonial attire and the posture of the dancers with a fair amount of accuracy. Interesting details include the spruce collars around the necks of Talking God and the Male Yeis, and the hair of the Female Yeis which flows down their backs.

The complex geometric border and the addition of decorative feathers in the field are characteristic of the more elaborate Yeibichai weavings of the 1920s.

12. Yeibichai Dancers

Although still fanciful, the portrayal of the dancers in this piece is somewhat more realistic than in the previous weavings. The masks are accurately represented with their blue paint and characteristic shapes. The Male Yeis, however, are shown not in their ritual white body paint, but instead in long-sleeved shirts which they would wear on extremely cold nights. The presence of birds, considered by the Navajos as harbingers of peace and happiness, constitutes a good omen. The interlacing meander design of the border is common in Navajo rugs woven between 1900 and 1930.

circa 1925
69″ x 53″
warps 9
wefts 34
handspun wool

13. Yeibichai Dancers

circa 1925
51″ x 37″
warps 8
wefts 26
handspun wool
commercial yarn

At first glance the dancers portrayed here appear similar, but on closer look, one discovers that the weaver has introduced great variation into their attire. Talking God (right) is depicted wearing a kilt, rather than the more common long pants. The most intriguing feature of this weaving, however, is the presence of two small children with square masks holding onto the skirts of the female dancers. This may be a reminder that the Nightway serves as an initiation ceremony for Navajo youngsters.

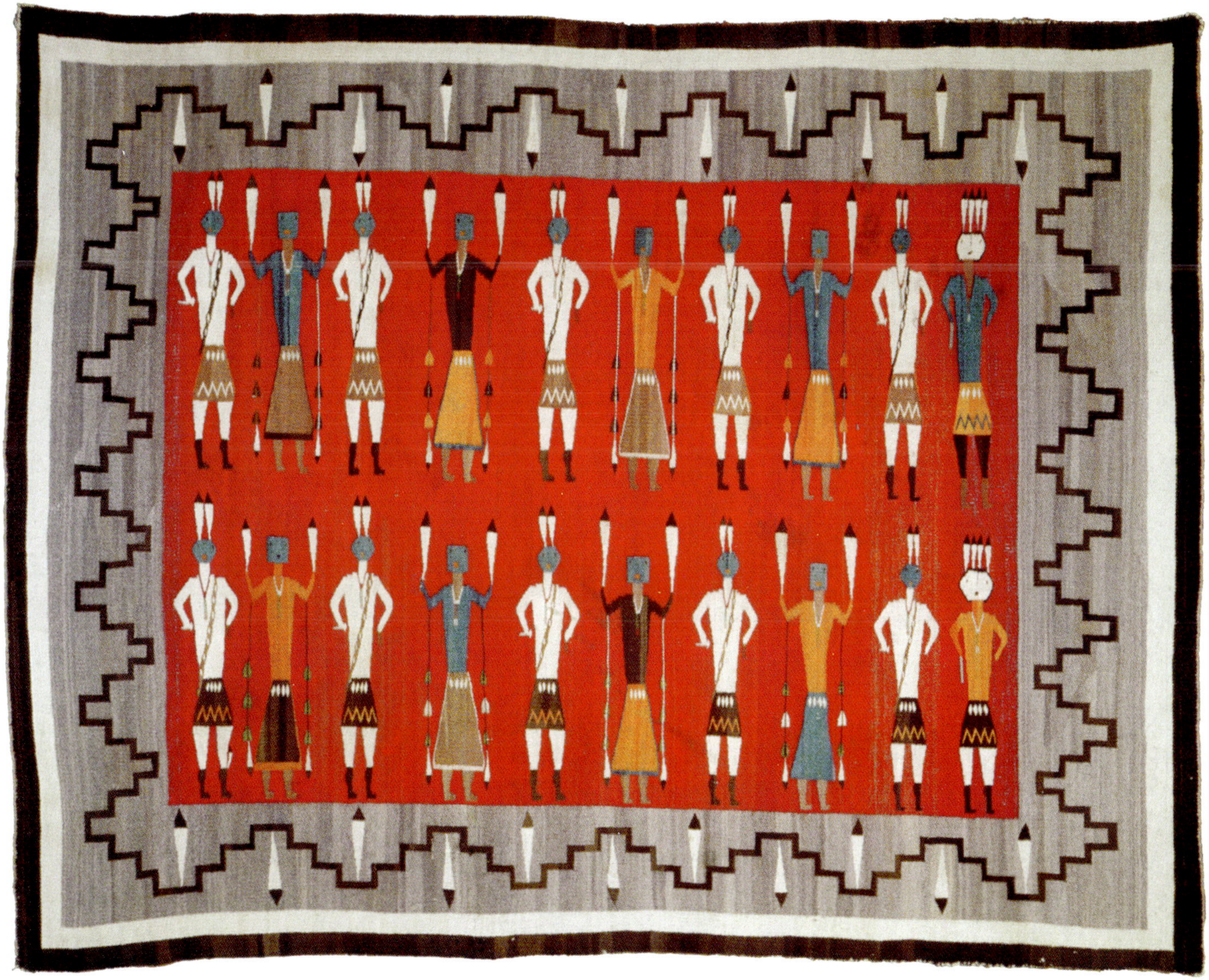

14. Yeibichai Dancers

This weaving is one of the few known early Yeibichai textiles featuring more than one team of dancers. Each of the two rows of alternating Male and Female Yeis is headed by Talking God, recognizable by his multi-feathered headdress. In spite of their small size, the dancers are portrayed in fine detail. The weaver has alternated the color of their attire so that they stand out clearly against the brilliant red background. The muted border draws the viewer's eye to the center of the scene.

circa 1920
73" x 48"
warps 9
wefts 30
handspun wool

All-Male Yeibichai Dance Teams: Standardization of Patterns

As a Yeibichai team enters the ceremonial ground, the dancers are in a single line of alternating Male and Female Yeis. This formation is maintained until a certain moment in the chant when the Male and Female divinities separate into two parallel lines of six dancers each (Matthews 1902:147-48). Early on, some weavers chose to represent the all-male line of dancers rather than the visually more interesting line of alternating men and women. The all-male pattern, since it was easier to reproduce, eventually prevailed. By 1935, it had been adopted by most weavers of Yeibichai textiles.

The early examples of weavings featuring all-male teams of dancers often have complex borders and include decorative elements such as feathers and rainbow bars in their fields. The figures represented vary in number, generally from 5 to 10, as well as in size, posture and ceremonial attire. As the all-male style developed, however, the patterns quickly became standardized.

The vast majority of Yeibichai weavings produced after 1935 have a plain field and a simple border consisting of a single black band. They feature six male dancers, identical in every respect except for small variations in the decoration of their kilts. Talking God is usually, but not always, included. While these later weavings often lack the spontaneity and originality so typical of the early textiles, they exhibit artistic qualities of their own. In the best examples, the weaving is fine and tighter than in the older pieces, the symmetrical composition is better balanced, and the design more focused. A richer palette enables the weavers to add color and variety to the ceremonial attire of the dancers. Large-size weavings containing up to 12 dancers continued to be made through the 1940s.

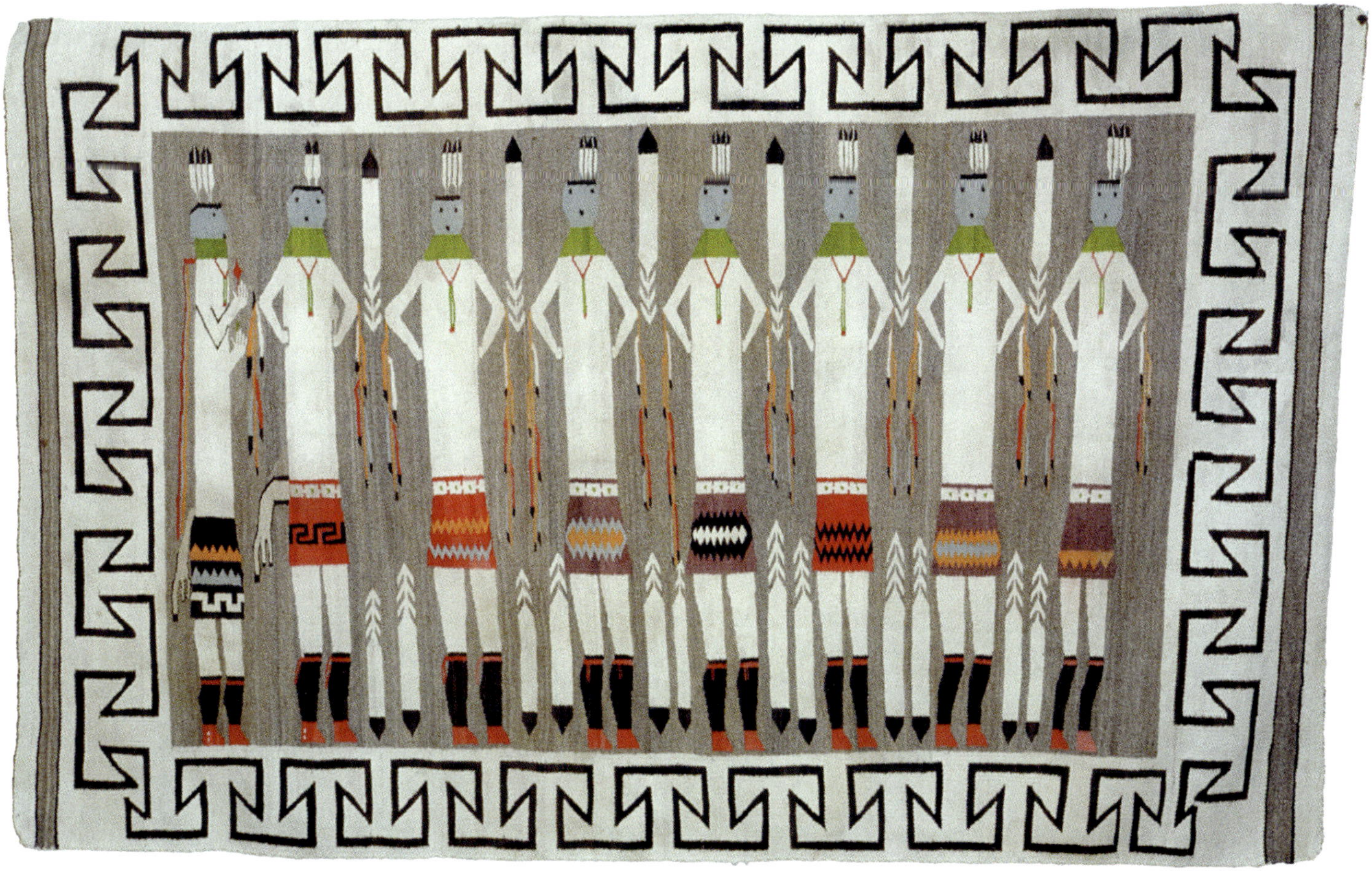

15. Yeibichai Dancers

This weaving features a well-balanced, simple design with a row of identical Male Yeis, thus foreshadowing the standard pattern that would be widely followed in the mid-1930s. The weaver apparently miscalculated the available space, but creatively managed to fit in an eighth dancer by making him thinner and presenting him in profile. Possibly to break the symmetry of the dancers, she added fox pelts to the kilts of the last two figures and omitted the large decorative feathers.

circa 1930
82″ x 52″
warps 9
wefts 30
handspun wool

16. Yeibichai Dancers

1935-1945
71" x 42"
warps 7
wefts 22
handspun wool

In this weaving, the portrayal of the Male Yeis is even more simplified than in the preceding example. As part of their cermonial attire, the dancers have colorful streamers hanging from their elbows. To represent these streamers, the weaver has used a beaded stitch typical of sashes woven on a belt loom. she has also added variety to the belts of the dancers, representing some with silver "butterfly" spanners between the large conchas with their turquoise stones.

17. Yeibichai Dancers

This well-woven but somewhat thick textile is a typical example of the Yeibichai rugs produced in the Lukachukai region. In spite of her naive style, the weaver represents the attire of the Male Yei dancers fairly accurately with their gourds and fox pelts. They are depicted wearing leather bandoleer straps across their torsos. These straps, decorated with silver buttons, are attached to leather pouches (not visible here) which Navajo men traditionally used to carry tobacco and small objects.

late 1930s
61″ x 35″
warps 8
wefts 30
handspun wool

18. Yeibichai Dancers

circa 1935
55″ x 38″
warps 11
wefts 35
handspun wool

The weaver of this piece has used the Yeibichai theme to create a simple but attractive tableau. The dancers are separated by stalks of corn, a plant considered sacred by the Navajos and often represented in their sandpaintings in the above manner with three roots and three tassels. The artistic talent of the weaver is evidenced by her tight control of space and the overall balance of her composition.

19. Yeibichai Dancers

In this intriguing piece, an assembly of Holy People watch a quintet of Yeibichai dancers, much as ordinary spectators would attend an open-air performance. The divinities are portrayed with their square heads placed atop clouds, symbolically represented as terraced blocks. In her design, the weaver has captured the essence of the Navajo curative ceremony which aims to attract the Holy People to the scene so that they can dispense their goodness on those present.

circa 1935
84″ x 57″
warps 6
wefts 24
handspun wool

Expressing the Movement of the Dance

In performing the Yeibichai dance, the masked god-impersonators execute a variety of steps as they get into different formations. They move forward in a single file, change directions, separate into two lines, regroup facing each other, and advance in pairs, Virginia Reel style (Matthews 1902:147-151). During these various dance segments, the impersonator of Water Sprinkler dances around mimicking the attitudes and steps of the others. The corresponding impression of movement and action is difficult to convey in a two-dimensional weaving, and especially in a woven textile where the artist is technically constrained by the linear orientation of her yarn. Her task is further complicated when she represents the dancers in a single row facing forward, as in the dominant Lukachukai style of Yeibichai textiles, since she cannot use the perspective effect of different planes to express their movement. Some especially gifted weavers successfully met the challenge by developing original ways to impart a feeling of motion and action, as seen in the textiles of this section.

20. Yeibichai Dancers

In this fanciful depiction of a Yeibichai dance team, all the male participants, including Talking God, are wearing white body paint and mini-kilts. The trailing figure on the left, holding a fox pelt in his hand, is the impersonator of Water Sprinkler, a figure rarely depicted in early Yeibichai weavings.

The female participants are much more staid in their long skirts and white leather leggings. The weaver has imparted a feeling of movement to the composition by placing the dancers on a slightly uneven plane and representing them with varied arm positions, raised feet and bent knees.

circa 1920
75″ x 35″
warps 7
wefts 26
handspun wool

21. Yeibichai Dancers

1920s
62″ x 38″
warps 9
wefts 32
handspun yarn

In this unconventional portrayal of the Yeibichai dance, the male participants wear their everyday clothing rather than ceremonial kilts and body paint. The weaver has used a rich palette of harmonious colors to highlight the individuality of each dancer. The forward movement and direction of the dance is suggested by the toe-down position of the dancers' feet. Water Sprinkler, the figure on the left, lets his fox pelt hang limp. However, the weaver has caught the upward swing of Talking God's squirrel bag in mid-air in a "stop-action" moment that we would associate more typically with photography.

22. Yeibichai Dancers

Early ethnologists reported that a woman would occasionally join the men in the Yeibichai dance, as seen in this weaving. Here she is shown in the traditional double manta dress that was worn by Navajo women until the 1890s. The weaver has skillfully conveyed the serpentine movement of the line of dancers by presenting the individual members from different angles: Talking God and the first two dancers are facing forward, the next three dancers are in profile, and the last figure is again facing forward. The border features a geometric design found in the prehistoric paintings in Canyon de Chelly.

1930s
67″ x 49″
warps 15
wefts 40
handspun yarn
commercial yarn

23. Yeibichai Dancers

1920-1930
79" x 35"
warps 6
wefts 30 - 40
handspun yarn

In this elongated weaving, the god impersonators are portayed against an unusual bright red background. The weaver has created a sense of perspective by giving the dancers slightly different sizes and by depicting them in different stances. Standing erect, the larger Female Yeis occupy the foreground of the scene. Thinner and with their knees bent, the Male Yeis seem to stand to the back. The diminuitive Water Sprinkler on the left recedes farther into the background.

24. Yeibichai Dancers in Pairs

In most Yeibichai weavings, the dancers are shown in a straight line, the way they enter the dance area at the beginning of their performance. During the dance, the Male and Female Yeis separate into two lines and then promenade in pairs in a formation that early ethnologists likened to the Virginia Reel. By representing her figures in couples and fancifully switching the positions of the first two dancers, the weaver has given an impression of action not found in the more conventional representations. In addition, she has placed a fifth dancer sideways at the top of the weaving, possibly to capture the moment when the lead dancer resumes his position at the back of the line. Another interesting feature of this weaving is the accurate rendering of the triangular shapes of the eyes as they are painted on the sacred masks.

1925-1935
81″ x 52″
warps 9
wefts 30
handspun yarn

Dancers in Profile

By portraying the dancers in profile, the weaver can represent their ceremonial attire in greater detail, especially the shapes of the headmasks, the decorations of the kilts, the gourd rattles and the fox pelts attached to the backs of their belts. Even more importantly, she can introduce perspective and a sense of forward movement by placing the feet of the dancers on two separate planes with one leg straight and the other slightly raised and bent at the knee. To reinforce the feeling of motion, she depicts the arms in two different positions: the right hand, which is shaking a gourd, rattle is higher than the left hand, which is holding a spruce branch.

Yeibichai weavings showing the dancers in profile are sometimes referred to as Gallegos or Simpson rugs, since this style was originated around 1910 by weavers living near the Gallegos Wash, south of Farmington, New Mexico, where Dick Simpson had his trading post (see Figure 12). Weavings in this style have a compact design. The early examples usually have a square format and feature two to four male dancers. A few rare pieces depict two superimposed rows of dancers. During the 1910-1950 period, this style was much less popular than the more prevalent Lukachukai pattern, in which the rows of dancers are facing forward. The profile design was revived in the 1940s and has become a common way of depicting the Yeibichai dance in modern weavings.

circa 1940
46″ x 48″
warps 9
wefts 28
handspun wool

25. Yeibichai Dancers

This profile weaving clearly shows how the masks of the Male Yeis are constructed. Each mask consists of two parts sewn together across the top and down the sides. The back is made of soft white doeskin and the front is made of white buckskin that has been dyed a turquoise blue using mineral pigments. Stitched across the top is a fringe of braided red wool or horsehair. Two eagle feathers are attached to the top right-hand side of the mask. The round mouthpiece, which may be either blunt or shaped like the beak of a bird (as in this weaving), is made from the neck of a gourd and functions as a breathing pipe. The base of the mouthpiece is decorated with brown downy owl feathers.

26. Yeibichai Dancers

1920s
25″ x 48″
warps 10
wefts 34
commercial yarn,
cotton warp

This very unusual tapestry combines elements of both the Lukachukai and Gallegos styles–the dancers are facing forward but their bodies are in partial profile. Like the Gallegos weavings, however, this piece was woven from the feet up. Distinctive details include the asymmetric border, the decorative geometric elements in the background, and the heavy emphasis on the dancers' jewelry. Twirls of wool protruding from the tops of masks add a third dimension to the composition. The exclusive use of commercial yarns is uncommon in Yeibichai weavings of the 1920s.

27. Yeibichai Dancers

Members of a Yeibichai team are attired in an identical manner except for their kilts which are often individualized, as in this weaving. The swastika symbol in the background is found on many pre-historic Native American artifacts. Because it symbolized good fortune and closely resembled a sandpainting figure known as "Whirling Logs," its reproduction in Navajo rugs and jewelry was highly encouraged by Indian traders in the early twentieth century. The symbol was abandoned in the 1930s when it became associated with Nazi Germany.

1920s
37″ x 39″
warps 8
wefts 30
handspun wool

28. Yeibichai Dancers

Because of strong technical and stylistic similarities, this fine tapestry is probably the work of the same woman who made the one on the facing page. Both pieces illustrate the high level of artistry reached by skillful and creative weavers in interpreting the Yeibichai theme. The presentation of the dancers in two groups, at different angles and facing in opposite directions, gives the scene a sense of perspective and an overall impression of movement. The outer border contains a series of stacked triangles that traditionally symbolize cloud formations in sandpainting designs.

1940s
52″ x 31″
warps 12
wefts 38
handspun wool,
commercial yarn

29. Yeibichai Dancers

The weaver of this piece has successfully placed two teams of Yeibichai dancers on a relatively small surface. The two lines face in opposite directions, suggesting two teams relaying one another in the course of the all-night performance of the sacred rite. In spite of the space constraints, the dancers are portrayed in great detail with long fox pelts and colored streamers dangling down their backs. The variety in the designs of the kilts and their brilliant coloring add to the overall attractiveness of this weaving.

1940s
69″ x 51″
warps 7
wefts 26
handspun wool,
commercial yarn

Yeibichai Dancers as Decorative Elements

In a typical Yeibichai textile, the line of masked god impersonators constitutes the main focus of the weaving and its only theme. Occasionally, however, Navajo women would insert figures of Yeibichai dancers as a decorative element or secondary theme of their composition. In some examples, the small figures are placed at the corners or scattered in the field of a plain geometric weaving. In other cases, they are incorporated into the designs of textiles woven in a distinctively "regional" style, such as Early Crystal, Two Grey Hills, or Storm Pattern. On even rarer occasions, weavers have combined Yeibichai dancers with other figurative elements to create totally idiosyncratic designs. The weavings resulting from these secondary treatments of the Yeibichai theme are unique pieces since none conforms to a pre-established style. Most of them were produced in the 1920s and 1930s when the Yeibichai genre of Navajo textiles attained the peak of its creativity.

1915-1925
65″ x 61″
warps 6
wefts 24
handspun wool

30. Yeibichai Dancers in a Cross-shape Weaving

Square crosses are frequently incorporated into the designs of Navajo weavings of the late nineteenth and early twentieth centuries. Textiles actually woven in the shape of a cross, however, are very uncommon, since the traditional Navajo loom is designed only for producing rectangular pieces.

The unusual character of this weaving is reinforced by the inclusion of five Yeibichai dancers placed in the four arms and in the center of the cross. The dark background may serve as a reminder that the Yeibichai dance is always performed in the middle of the night.

31. Yeibichai Dancers around a Geometric Field

In its general appearance, this weaving is typical of the fairly standard pan-Reservation rugs produced in the period between 1925 and 1940. Its central design, reminiscent of a large hourglass, can be found as a decorative element in many of these rugs. The sobriety of the colors, limited to the natural shades of sheep's wool with the addition of aniline red, is also characteristic of the period.

The originality of this piece lies in the two bands of four Yeibichai dancers placed at the top and bottom of the weaving. Disposing of a limited palette, the weaver has used different shades of beige to represent the spruce collars of the dancers as well as their fox pelts.

1925-1940
75" x 43"
warps 7
wefts 28
handspun wool

32. Yeibichai Dance Scene within a Rug

In this rug-within-a-rug weaving, the four male Yeibichai dancers, each with a leather bandoleer pouch across his chest, are performing in the sandy dance arena. Talking God stands to the right of the scene and Water Sprinkler, impersonated by a young teenager, stands to the left, shaking a white fox pelt. The amount of $1000, naively written backwards, might simply be a decorative element or perhaps a very optimistic indication of how much money the weaver hoped to be paid by the trader. Probably the weaver received about $50 or at most $100.

1920-1935
103" x 70"
warps 7
wefts 18
handspun wool

33. Two Grey Hills Yeibichai

circa 1925
90″ x 53″
warps 10
wefts 38
handspun wool

Two Grey Hills textiles are characterized by a very fine weave, a muted palette limited to the natural colors of the wool, and a carefully organized symmetrical design consisting of a dominant central panel with secondary motifs displayed in the four corners. The Storm Pattern design and the central eight-pointed star are typically found in textiles woven between 1920 and 1930. What makes this Two Grey Hills weaving unusual, and possibly unique, is the incorporation of two symmetrical pairs of Yeibichai dancers within its design. The male dancer in each pair can easily be identified by his tall stature, as well as by his two feather headdress and rattle. All four dancers are portrayed with fingers, a detail which many weavers often omit for fear of rendering sacred figures too accurately.

34. Yeibichai Dancers in a Sandpainting-type Weaving

In the 1920s, several weavers in the Lukachukai area created fanciful textiles that intermingled Yeibichai figures with design elements borrowed from sandpainting designs. Here the central cross delineates the background for two rows of alternating male and female Yeibichai dancers. The stooped figure on the bottom left is the impersonator of Humpback God who plays a minor role in the Nightway ceremony, but does not appear in the Yeibichai dance of the last night. The central field is bordered by two black figures that resemble the "Rainbow Guardians" of certain Nightway sand-paintings. The openings between the Guardians are protected by bows, arrows, and Water Creatures.

1920s
73″ x 50″
warps 8
wefts 28
handspun wool

35. Corn Yei with Yeibichai Dancers

Along with beans, tobacco and squash, corn is one of the four sacred plants of the Navajo. Its personified form, represented in sandpainting designs as Corn People or Corn Yeis, consists of a stylized cornstalk with a square human head. Here the Corn Yei is shown upside down, with its head in the ground and its three white roots in the air. At the top and bottom of the scene, the weaver has added four small female dancers with feathered masks in the Yei style. The broad border contains 45 small birds, often considered to be symbols of good fortune.

1915-1925
77" x 46"
warps 9
wefts 30
handspun wool

36. Yeibichai Dancers around a Corn Yei

The central figure is an elongated Corn Yei with 16 leaf-arms, flanked on each side by a row of six Yeibichai dancers. These dancers, who are depicted arms akimbo in the typical Yeibichai stance, are rendered with a minimum of detail. Birds of different sizes, hues and plumage are commonly included in Corn Yei weavings. Here they are randomly arranged to fill in the background, rather than being neatly perched on the leaves of the corn plant. Five stylized otters which act as protective guardians in Navajo sand-paintings have been placed in the corners of the weaving.

1930s
87″ x 47″
warps 8
wefts 30
handspun wool

37. Yeibichai Dancers with Cars and Buildings

1920s
77" x 37"
warps 8
wefts 24
handspun wool,
commercial yarn

Navajo weavings seldom contain symbols from both the spiritual (Navajo) world and the material (Anglo) world. Here the weaver has combined these elements to evoke two cultures with radically different concepts of life, but who are curious about each other. The upper part, consisting of four female Yeibichai dancers separated by stylized otters, symbolizes the Navajo culture. The Anglo culture is evoked in the lower part by two-story buildings representing the vocational boarding schools that the Bureau of Indian Affairs built on the Reservation for Navajo children. The black cars with their protruding radiator caps and exterior spare tires resemble the "Indian Detour" cars which the Fred Harvey Company used in the 1920s to transport groups of tourists across the Navajo Reservation to the Hopi mesas.

1915-1935
39″ x 53″
warps 5
wefts 28
handspun wool

38. Franciscan Priest with Yei-style Dancers

This unique ecumenical textile portrays a Catholic monk flanked by two Yei-style dancers. This peaceful composition may evoke the good relations between the Franciscan priests of Saint Michaels Mission in Arizona and their Navajo neighbors. The Yei-like dancers have four-pointed Navajo stars on their heads, but carry wands with five-pointed Christian or Western stars. The Franciscan monk, holding aloft two white crosses, wears his traditional hooded robe, belted with a white cord to which is attached a wooden rosary. The three central figures do not seem at all perturbed by the presence of the dark snake which in both Christian and Navajo cultures symbolizes malevolent power.

Other Ceremonial Dancers

Weavers have sometimes departed from the Yeibichai dance theme to portray participants in other Navajo sacred rituals. Weavings like the one on the right which features Nightway god impersonators other than Yeibichai dancers are extremely rare. Other esoteric weavings contain figures that very distantly evoke performers in the Mountain-Shootingway ceremony. Like the Nightway, this Navajo ceremony takes place during the winter months when snakes and bears are hibernating. It also lasts for nine days and culminates on the last night in a spectacular grand finale known as the Corral Dance, during which acts of magic are performed. In some textiles with ceremonial dancers, the figures are so stylized that they cannot be associated with any specific ritual and should instead be considered as fanciful products of the weaver's imagination.

1920s
32″ x 31″
warps 6
wefts 24
handspun wool

39. Nightway Divinities

During the nine days of the Nightway ceremony, different god impersonators perform rites of succor for the benefit of the patient. Except for Talking God, also known as Yeibichai, the leader of the Yeis, these divinities do not participate in the dance of the last night. In this textile, the weaver has portrayed Talking God, recognizable by his multi-feathered headdress and the spotted Abert squirrel bag in his hand, accompanied by the impersonator of Fringed Mouth God (middle) and Monster Slayer (left). Monster Slayer is the War God whom the Navajos revere as their divine protector.

1930s
54″ x 51″
warps 9
wefts 26
handspun wool

40. Stylized Dancers

This intriguing type of rug with its esoteric figures began to appear in the 1920s and continued to be woven until the 1950s, probably by a single family of weavers. The distinctive characteristic of these rugs lies in the representation of the human face with its clearly delineated features: eyes, eyebrows, mouth, and often nostrils. Since they are portrayed without masks, these figures are not Yeibichai dancers although their attire is generally similar: body paint, colorful ceremonial kilts, streamers with tassles hanging from their elbows, and woolen leggings with red garters.

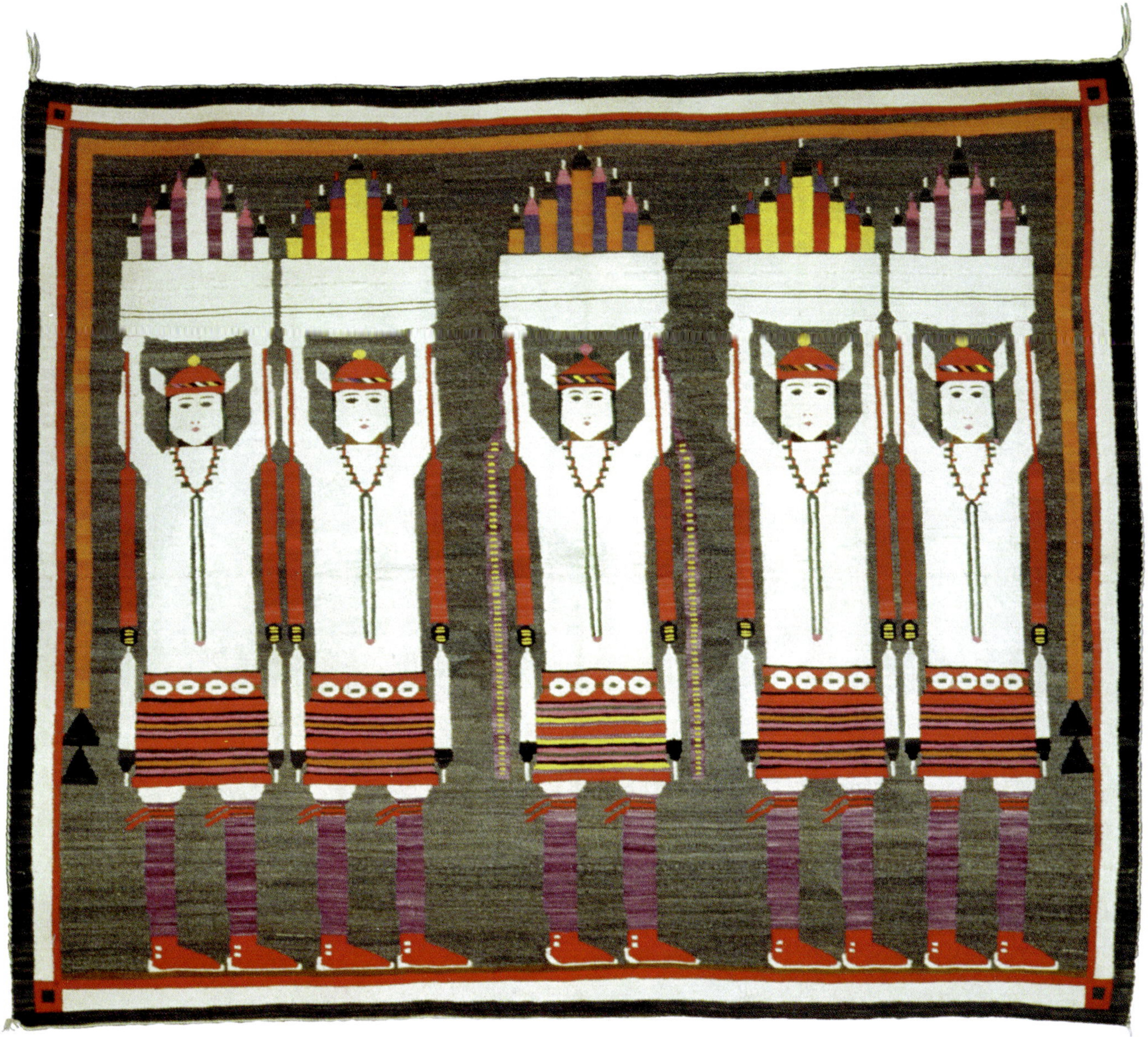

41. Mountain-Shootingway Dancers

The unmasked Mountain-Shootingway dancers in this weaving are readily identified by their distinctive red wool hats decorated with buffalo horns. Above their heads, the dancers hold fanciful hoops with upright eagle feathers that seem to be reflecting the yellow and orange flames of the bonfires. The dark background of the weaving evokes the nighttime atmosphere of the ceremony.

This textile was probably produced by the same family who created the rug on the left. The design was woven vertically on an exceptionally broad loom measuring over seven feet in width.

1925-1935
70″ x 83″
warps 9
wefts 24
handspun wool

42. Mountain-Shootingway Dancers

1925-1935
110″ x 55″
warps 7
wefts 28
handspun wool

This weaving portrays two simultaneous but distinct dances, one in the center of the rug and the other around the border, thus giving the scene a sense of circular motion. With their characteristic red pointed hats with white eagle feathers, the figures in the central field evoke the dancers who perform on the last night of the Mountain-Shootingway ceremony.

The dancers forming the border are distantly reminiscent of the performers in the Apache Mountain Spirit Dance who carry wooden wands, often with cross-sticks, and wear wooden headdresses. In designing the border, the weaver also created a reverse black pattern that resembles a row of ceremonial hide rattles.

Bibliography

Amsden, Charles Avery
1934 *Navajo Weaving: Its Technic and History.* Fine Arts Press, Santa Ana, CA. [Reprinted in 1975 by Peregrine Smith, Salt Lake City, UT.]

Blomberg, Nancy
1990 "Sacred Figures in Navajo Blankets: A Re-evaluation of Time Frame and its Implication for Cultural Change", *Kiva,* 55:357-372.

Campbell, Tyrone and Joel and Kate Kopp
1991 *Navajo Pictorial Weaving 1880-1950.* Dutton Studio Books, New York, NY.

Coolidge, Dane and Mary Roberts Coolidge
1930 *The Navajo Indians.* Houghton Mifflin Company, Boston, MA.

Curtis, Edward S.
1907 *Apache, Jicarilla Apache, Navajo. The North American Indian.* Vol. 1. The University Press, Cambridge, MA.

Fane, Diana, Ira Jacknis and Lise M. Breen
1991 *Objects of Myth and Memory: American Indian Art at The Brooklyn Museum.* University of Washington Press, Seattle, WA.

Faris, James C.
1990 *The Nightway: A History and a History of Documentation of a Navajo Ceremonial.* University of New Mexico Press, Albuquerque, NM.

Garrigan, John
1981 *Southwestern Weaving from the Collection of the Stark Museum of Art.* Stark Foundation, Orange, TX.

Haile, Berard
1947 *Head and Face Masks in Navaho Ceremonialism.* St. Michaels Press, St. Michaels, AZ. [Reprinted in 1996 by the University of Utah Press, Salt Lake City, UT.]

Hedlund, Ann Lane
1997 *Navajo Weaving from the Santa Fe Collection, 1971-1996.* National Cowboy Hall of Fame, Oklahoma City, OK 73111.

James, George Wharton
1914 *Indian Blankets and Their Makers.* A.C. McClury & Co., Chicago, IL. [Reprinted in 1974 by Dover Publications, New York, NY.]

Long, Paul V.
1992 *Big Eyes: The Southwestern Photographs of Simeon Schwemberger, 1902-1908.* University of New Mexico Press, Albuquerque, NM.

Matthews, Washington
1902 *The Night Chant. A Navaho Ceremony.* Knickerbocker Press, New York, NY. [Reprinted in 1995 by the University of Utah Press, Salt Lake City, UT.]

Newcomb, Franc Johnson
1964 *Hosteen Klah, Navaho Medicine Man and Sand Painter.* University of Oklahoma Press, Norman, OK.

Ortiz, Alfonso
1983 *Handbook of North American Indians, Vol. 10: Southwest*, Smithsonian Institute, Washington, DC.

Parezo, Nancy J.
1983 *Navajo Sandpainting: From Religious Art to Commercial Art.* University of New Mexico Press, Albuquerque, NM.

Reichard, Gladys A.
1934 *Spider Woman: A Story of Navajo Weavers and Chanters.* Macmillan, New York, NY. [Reprinted by the University of New Mexico Press, Albuquerque, NM, 1992.]
1936 *Navajo Shepherd and Weaver*, J. J. Augustin, New York, NY. [Reprinted in 1974 as *Weaving a Navajo Blanket* by Dover Publications, New York, NY.]

Rodee, Marian
1987 *Weaving of the Southwest from the Maxwell Museum of Anthropology, University of New Mexico.* Schiffler Publishing, West Chester, PA.
1995 *One Hundred Years of Navajo Rugs.* University of New Mexico Press, Albuquerque, NM.

Bibliography continued

Schaafsma, Polly
1992 *Rock Art in New Mexico.* Museum of New Mexico Press, Santa Fe, NM.

Stevenson, James
1891 "Ceremonial of Hasjelti Dailjis and Mythical Sand Painting of the Navajo Indians," *Eighth Annual Report of the Bureau of Ethnology to the Secretary of the Smithsonian Institution, 1886-1887*, pp. 229-285. Government Printing Office, Washington, DC.

Valette, Jean-Paul and Rebecca M. Valette
1997 "In Search of Yah-nah-pah: The Early Gallegos 'Yei' Weavers and their Blankets, *American Indian Art Magazine*, 23(1):56-69.

Valette, Rebecca M. and Jean-Paul Valette
2000 "The Life and Work of Clitso Dedman, Navajo Woodcarver (1879?-1953)," *American Indian Art Magazine*, 25(2):54-67.

Washburn, Dorothy K., ed.
1984 *The Elkus Collection: Southwestern Indian Art.* California Academy of Sciences, San Francisco, CA.

Wyman, Leland C.
1983 *Southwest Indian Drypainting.* School of American Research, Santa Fe, NM..

Credits: Sources of Illustrations

Figure 1. (p. 7) Photo by Ben Wittick, courtesy of Museum of New Mexico (Santa Fe, NM), Neg. # 16466.
Figure 2. (p. 8) Photo by Bortell, courtesy of Museum of New Mexico (Santa Fe, NM), Neg. # 91045.
Figure 3. (p. 9) Courtesy School of American Research, Indian Arts Research Center (Santa Fe, NM), Cat. # IAF.P64.
Figure 4. (p. 10) Published in Edward S. Curtis, *Apache, Jicarilla Apache, Navajo. The North American Indian.,Vol. 1* (Cambridge, MA: The University Press, 1907).
Figure 5. (p. 10) Courtesy of Brooklyn Museum of Art Archives (Brooklyn, NY), *Culin Archival Collection, Report on a Collecting Trip Among the Indians of Calilfornia and Vancouver Island, May through October, 1908*, p. 6a.
Figure 6. (p. 11) Photo by Dong Lin, courtesy of California Academy of Sciences (San Francisco, CA), Ruth and Charles de Young Elkus Collection, Cat. # 0370-503 A to P.
Figure 7. (p. 12) Photo by Stephen Vedder (Boston College Audiovisual Services).
Figure 8. (p. 14) Photo by Michal Hardoof-Raz (Boston College Audiovisual Services).
Figure 9. (p. 15) Photo by Stephen Vedder (Boston College Audiovisual Services).
Figure 10. (p. 16) Photo by Rebecca M. Valette, courtesy of California Academy of Sciences (San Francisco, CA), Ruth and Charles de Young Elkus Collection, Cat. # 0370-0703.
Figure 11. (p. 17) Photo by Dale W. Anderson (Aztec Media), courtesy of Notah Dineh Museum (Cortez, CO).
Figure 12. (p. 17) Courtesy of Stark Museum of Art (Orange, TX), Cat # 82.900/59.
Figure 13. (p. 18) Courtesy of Museum of New Mexico (Santa Fe, NM). Neg. # 14288 (detail).
Figure 14. (p. 21) Map by Michael Rizzo, Museum of Our National Heritage (Lexington, MA).